# all

# the

# wild

# flowers

*c. westman*

stay wild

To all the wild flowers,

This book is simple, uncomplicated, and brief. You may even eventually gather I'm joking about 90% of the time - it's a humorous look at language and how society perceives identity through our limited vocabulary.

Um - what the heck am I talking about? That's not an explanation.

Yeah, true. But what more can I say - I just wrote the thing and now I gotta explain it.

Anyway, perhaps you may call this a meta-minimalist approach to poetry and prose. I might prefer the term, "thinking out loud and regretting it." In fact, I just made both of those up - so whatever.

But it is worth noting how society worships women - femaleness — in such bizarre ways and then tries to describe femininity in equally absurd ways. You know what I'm talking about – I don't think I really need to explain that. So, then I got to thinking, hmm, I suppose you could compare women to flowers and vice versa (Yeah, I actually thought that).

Maybe you can better understand what I'm saying when you read the book. It seems we're really talking about femininity here, and what we consider to be feminine. I don't know - my head's starting to spin just thinking about it.

So, here it is! I hope you appreciate its simplicity, and the minimalism of it. I feel it's needed in such complicated times. I also hope you enjoy the departure from tradition and know it's always okay to throw away the rules.

c. westman

delicate

fragile

weak

attractive

pretty

quiet

beautiful

silent

breakable

sensitive

emotional

too expensive

replaceable

too difficult to tend to

too hard to keep

all dried up

too many to choose from

too sweet

lovely

precious

too much

too smelly

too ugly

prickly when left untrimmed


Strangely, the same words are often equally

applied to flowers. Mull that over for a

while ...

anatomy
of a
flower

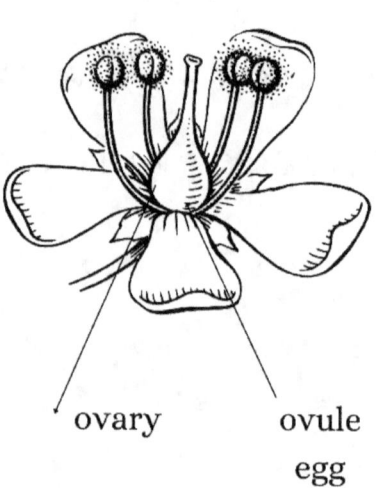

ovary          ovule

egg

Words &

stuff

# weak

who you callin' weak?

## weak

to be weak

is to be thought of as useless

as though a person is only as good

as how much they can carry

yet women carry human beings

in their wombs

-how much can you carry

for 9 months straight?


while a flower can hold

its weight in rainwater

and feed many beings

from the pollen it bears

- when was the last time

you fed the hungry?

resilient

resilience

a flower can weather many storms
and will not so much as bend
let alone break

when's the last time
you stood out in the rain
on a cold and stormy night
without needing an umbrella?

just sayin'

fragile

## fragility

is often a word used to describe someone

who is breakable

physically, mentally, and emotionally


Yet many things

which are fragile

are really just precious

like some fine chinaware

your favorite glass

filled with wine

a coffee mug

or the male ego

for instance


— mmm wine

wild

## wild

is a word to describe someone who

goes against the grain

used to condemn them for acting out

breaking the rules

a rebel

without a cause

defiant

disobedient

yet

free


- freeeeedom!

# broken

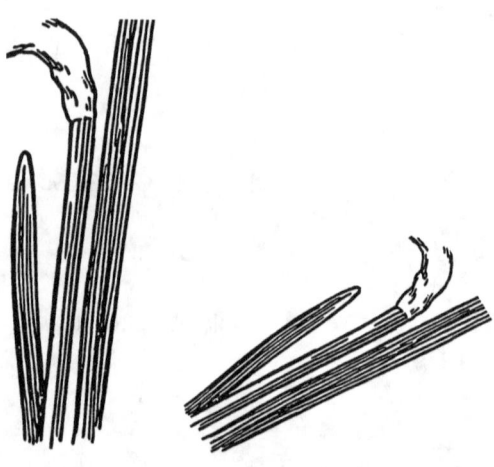

-   so, this kinda hurts

## to be broken

speaks to those who understand the true

nature of pain

to be hurt by someone you love

snapped in two and left for dead

whoa there...

dramatic much?

although your body may someday break

may your spirit be strong

but your drink be stronger

—

beautiful

**beautiful**

is considered a compliment

until it isn't

dirty

## dirty

there is nothing dirtier than simply the

word

itself

often meant to convey

shame or suggestion

a sexual connotation


but if it could be seen simply

for what it is

we would recognize it as

just meaning dirt -

that which comes from mother earth

from all that is natural

as pure as being born of a woman

or a flower that grows from her soil

too

skinny

## skinny

a person lacking in

substance

in primarily food

no tits

no ass

not enough

junk

or meat on the bones

a girl more or less

perhaps even a boy

too thin

to hold onto

—

are you healthy?

that's really all that matters

# quiet

- shhh, it's preferred you say nothing at all

## quiet

silent and still are synonyms

to mean a lack of sound

voiceless

as a young lady

somewhere

sits at the table

and is told

to be quiet

sensitive

is thought to be someone

who suffers from emotion

who is too soft

too serious

too much

why can't you just

get it together

be a man


toughen up

or lighten up

or make it easier for me

to be around you

-   too busy  livin' my best life

devoid of feelings!

# sensitive

- stop being so sensitive

tall

**too tall**

ladies

could you stop growing please?

you are making men feel small

while the world worships supermodels

six feet tall

then puts women in six-inch heels

and tells them not to

fall

over

—

got growing pains

&

stretch marks for days

prickly

### prickly

shave your goddamned legs

and your prickly temperament

while you're at it

tone it down

trim it all away

—

just grow a moustache already

c. westman

# plastic

## plastic

Could be described as being

as fake as a

hollywood romance

or as long lasting

as a divorce

- don't plant plastic flowers

is this really a flower

just because it says it is?

# natural

- maybe she's born with it

# intense

# stuff

some serious poems

coming up

we are not safe

where we are chosen

only for our beauty

# a world without flowers

it's hard to imagine a world without flowers

yet we continue to pick them superficially

we degrade their bodies

by cutting off their stems

trading mutilation for beauty

then turn around

and judge them

for their scars

for bearing stretch marks

preferring  plastic

flowers

that never age

that never change

not seeing

how we hurt them so

# we are the wildflowers

we

are

the

wild

flowers

who live not with regret

but chaos and whimsy

promiscuity

with no thought

nor care nor mercy


our spirit floats

past your garden

thankful to never be chosen

to be bought

with no dignity

we

are

the

wild

flowers

who wander freely

who go dancing in your fields

when you're asleep


we steal your memories

watching them like tv

in the shadows

etched within your mind

whispering for you

to leave the world behind

with all its ideals and fantasies

and just let go

## stolen flowers

stolen flowers go missing

from their homes

often taken from the wild

caught out in the darkness

alone

their pollen floats past prairie fields

where farmers plow and policemen know

they can steal flowers there

on stolen land or anywhere

they choose

but no one seems to care

we all say sorry

while no one seems to care

no one seems to care

no one seems to care

c. westman

in memory of the indigenous women and
children of Canada

you broke me in two

&

then left me to die

broken

flowers

everywhere

broken people too

watch where you step

# sittin pretty

they place you on a shelf

where you will remain

in a vase

in a room

locked into your role

until you

die

you pick women

like flowers

too many to choose from

there's always a better option

swipe left

swipe right

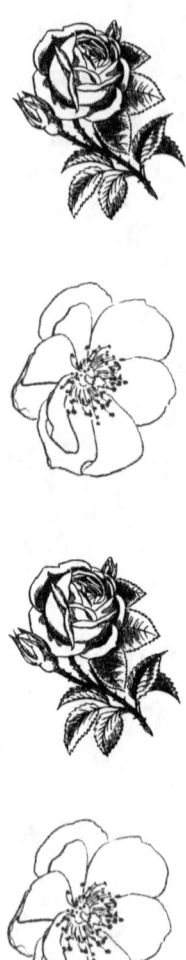

you smell good

look

don't touch

it hurts when you

handle me

that way

(deflowering)

adored

objectified

used

thrown out

they despise us

for our beauty

delicate

caption this

stop

staring

you are making me uncomfortable

did she ask

or did you

feel entitled

to tell her

has anyone ever told you

how pretty you are?

-   no, omg, it's the first time ever!

just let it

flow

*c. westman*

remember how

strong you are

# damaged

-  i want a refund

*c. westman*

if i wait until

the sun comes up

i may never be free

(domestic violence is never okay)

don't drink

boiled water

if you don't wanna get burned

how can you

cut me down to size

and then expect me to stay?

you're cut off

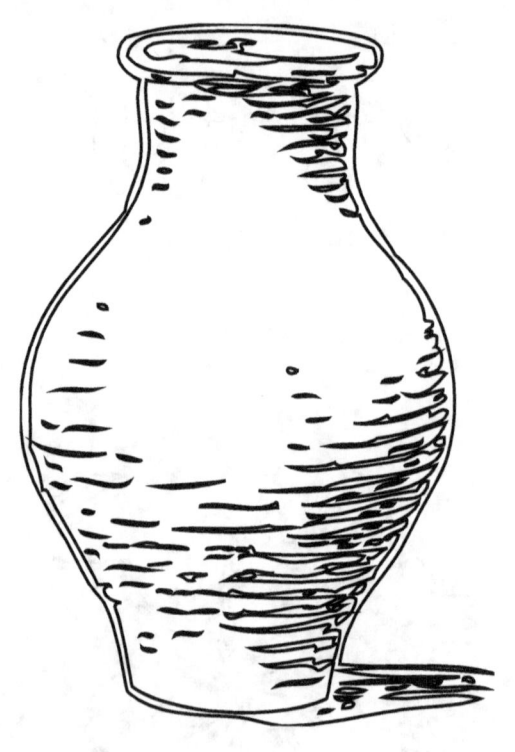

silent

you are not a prisoner

but a living

breathing

being

constantly

told to sit still

&

be happy

- smile

just because

they like you

doesn't mean

they respect you

if you could choose...

which flower

would you be?

love

&

heartbreak

we

are

all

delicate

flowers

waiting on

our leaves

to wilt

our stems

to break

# cute & quirky

on chilly days

tucked into bed

we shiver

the night

we shiver

the day

longing for warmth

of another to keep us safe

to call us by our name

thankful you are near

hopeful you will stay

ever knowing you won't last

# curvy

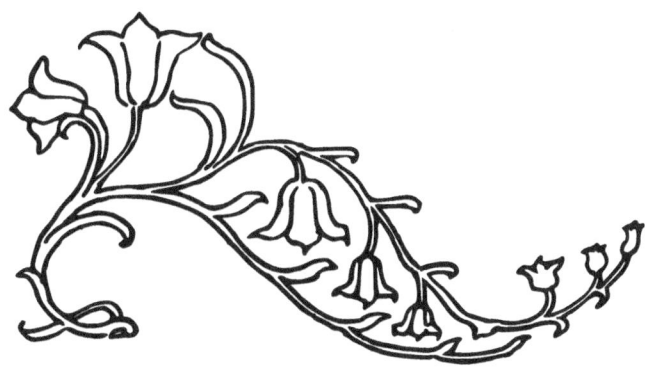

*c. westman*

keep growing

without him

he was never

going to keep you

sweet

you told me

you loved me

then tossed me

away

let my petals fall

and love me anyway

sad & lonely

a million weeds

are worthy

and so are you

perhaps

we all need air

i need space

perhaps

we all need love

i need water

hold me like

i could break

thirsty

c. westman

all

the

wild

flowers

wander

in the dark

looking for water

searching

for something

they go hunting

for the light

they go searching

for a home


all

the

wild

flowers

wander

in the dark

in the night

looking for something

searching

for

you

- soulmates

and so you remain

as you've always been

carrying a bouquet

down the aisle

of

*c. westman*

busting seams

white flashing lights

daydreams

in this nightmare

where you learn

to save yourself

then

a petal dies

and

a leaf does fall

each time

i hear his name

whispered upon

a stranger's lips

*c. westman*

# like poison to water

a kiss so sweet

the taste

of betrayal

is upon me

it runs rivers wide

and six feet deep

i am drowning in your lies

the liquor you call water

you are poison to my veins

but i can't

leave

let me go

well, that was

intense...

sexy

stuff

watch my petals

as they fall

to your floor

wet & waiting

love me

then

leave me

exposed

thorns and all

pick me

choose me

then take me home

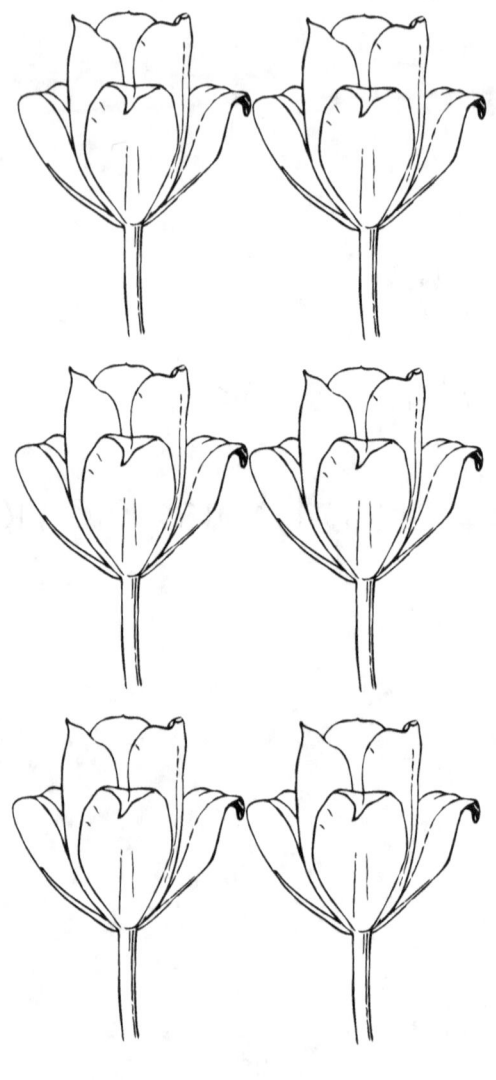

stacked

sensual

i crave the scent of spring on

my body

the dew of morning inside me

the sun's rays upon my flesh

— temptation

if a flower could speak
it'd sound like you


if it had hands
it'd touch me like you


and i would spend the night

hot

you

are

the

wildest

of

flowers

your

scent

is

inside

me

used up

dried out

*c. westman*

it's okay to be

as you've always been

just a

wild

flower

dancing naked

in the wind

bring me water

let me stay a while

longer

bring me to your knees

and i am whole

*c. westman*

in the bedroom of your bones

lays a woman for you there

with whiskey on her breath

and flowers in her hair

waiting patiently

for you

to come

home

More

words &

stuff

*fu

how many must you ~~pick~~

before you commit?

thick

blossom and bloom

blossom and bloom


day in and day out


until the water runs dry

until the water runs out


-   mothering

*c. westman*

don't look towards

the sun or you'll go blind

# Calm

passive

strong

for a woman

# this part is

# a bit

# depressing...

on aging and deat

old & ugly

there's only

limited time

before you

dry

up

where do flowers go

when they die?

some

flowers

flourish


others

just

wither

away

going grey

your weeds

are starting

to show

### a fall from grace

a flower's petals will someday fall

from grace

as flesh and bone

reckoning a mortal's song

inching back towards

the night unknown

to where you too shall go

lookin' good

for your age

aren't we all

just a bunch of

wild

flowers

waiting

on the sun?

a flower

is no more worthy

of life

than you

no less

nobody knows

where all the wildflowers go

long after they've gone

and said goodbye

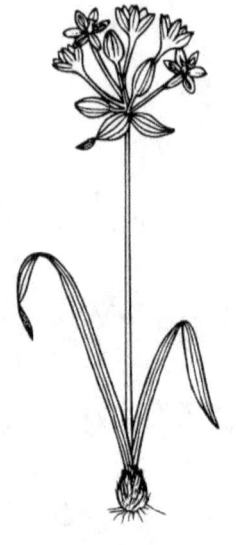

too old for this shit

life is life

and so it goes

let it take you like an echo

through the valleys

and down the fields

of yesterdays

and lost tomorrows

*c. westman*

**and so I creep**
through the valley
i go searching for your light
i hold my hand out to your soul
and gently whisper to the night
let me go
let me go


take me to the place
where he's living
where he's living
where he's gone to
where he's been


and so i creep
through the valley

waiting on a sign

by the wayside

through the valley

to the spirit

of your mind

## already gone

long before you remember

what you've lost

it has already passed you by

it has slipped through

the cracks

of space and time

then a breeze is felt

far and wide

and your whisper

reminds me how

i love you

Thank you to the artists who generously contributed their art. You can find all of these beautiful sketches online, please visit the website Pixabay, type in flower designs and the artist's pseudonym: openclipart-Vectors, all these images will appear.


Thank you to all who saw me through.

c. westman

all the wild flowers